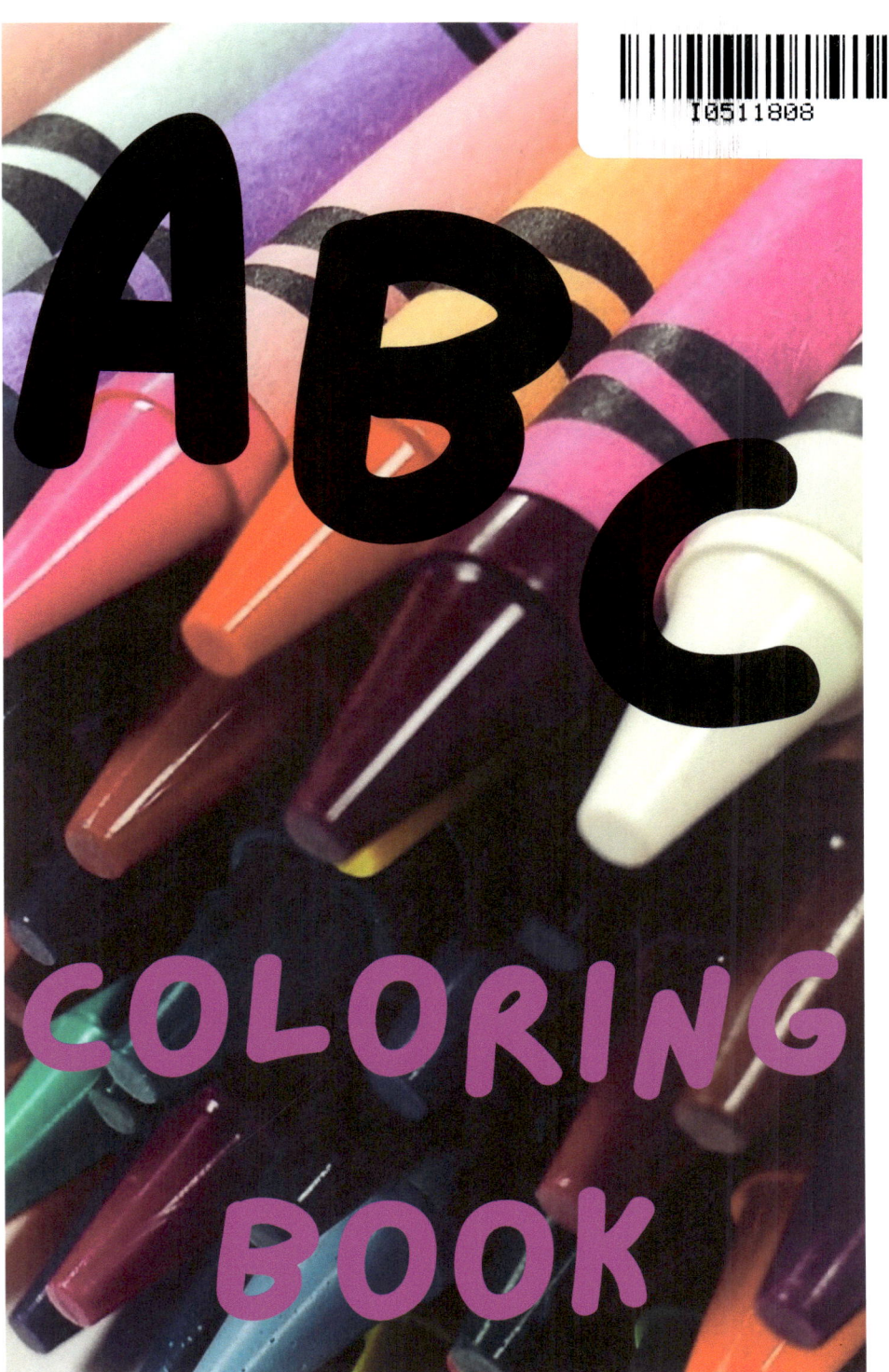

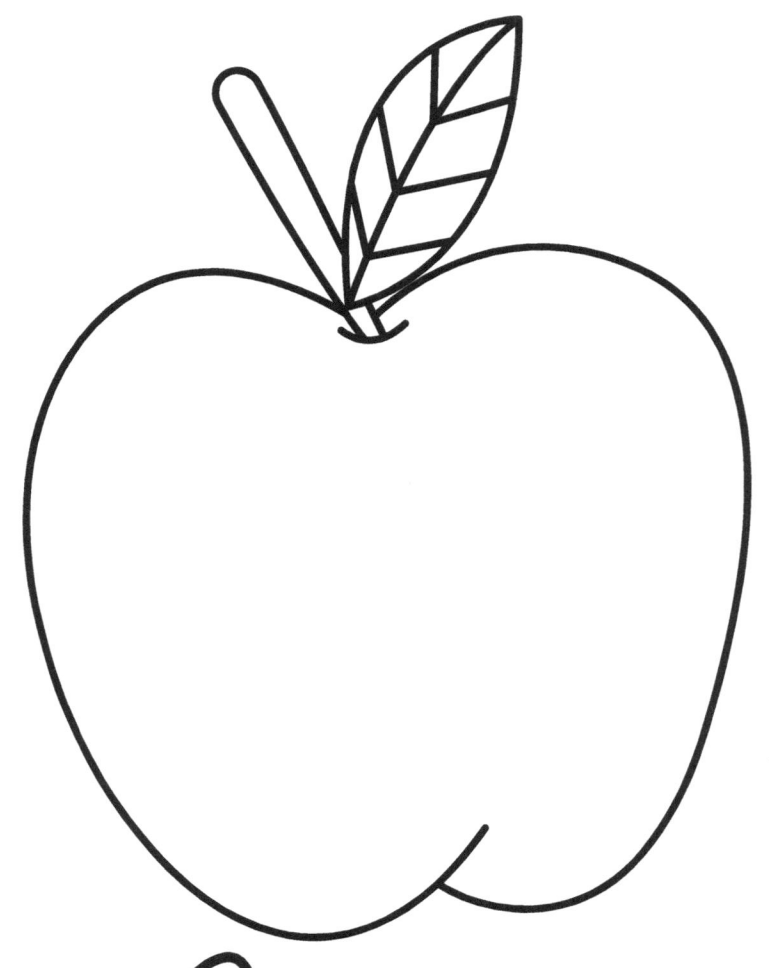

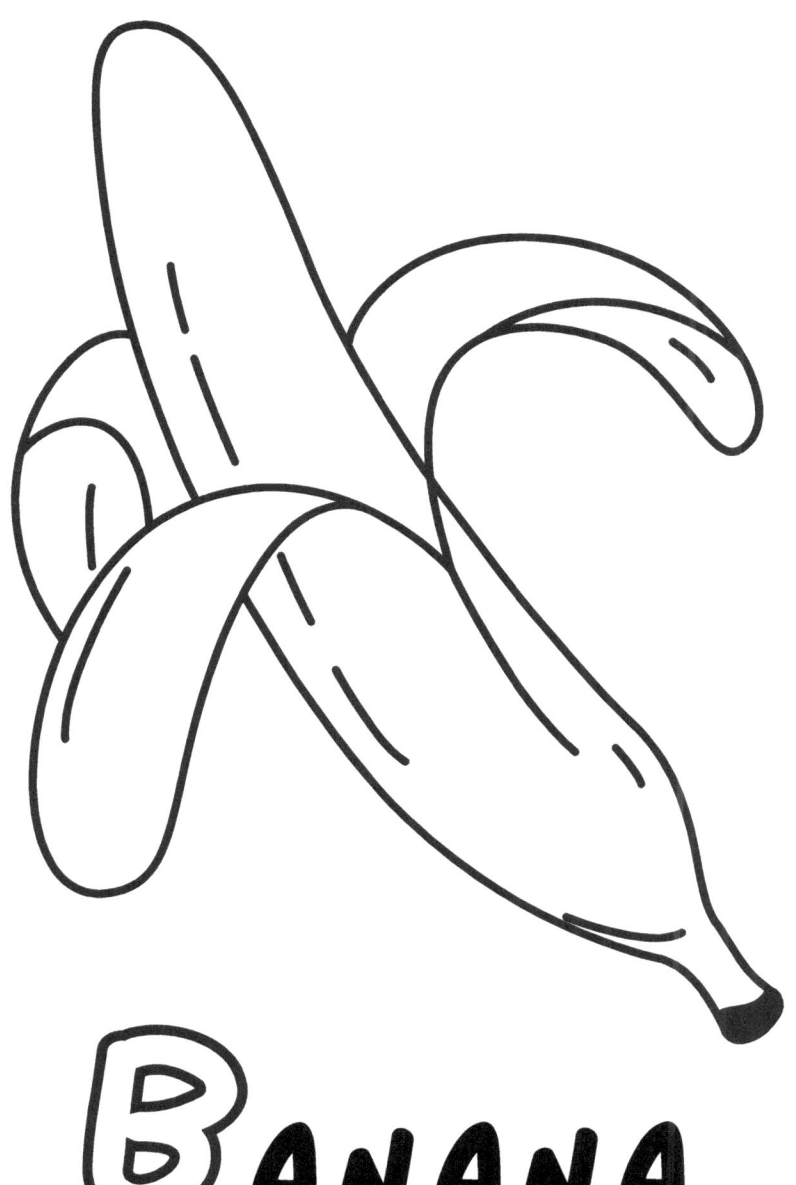

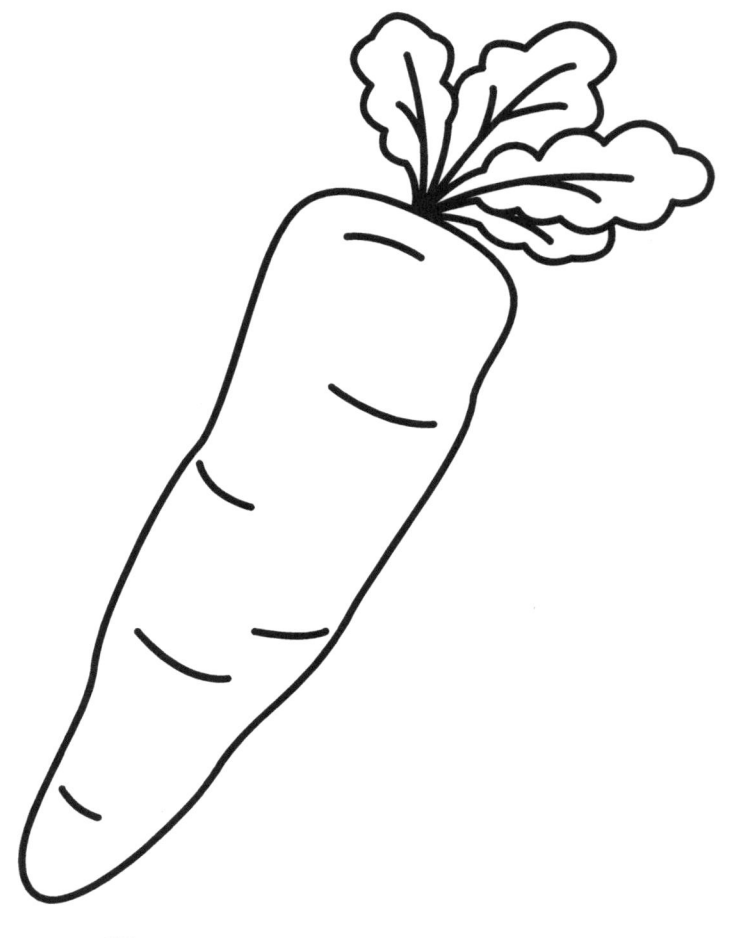

Carrot

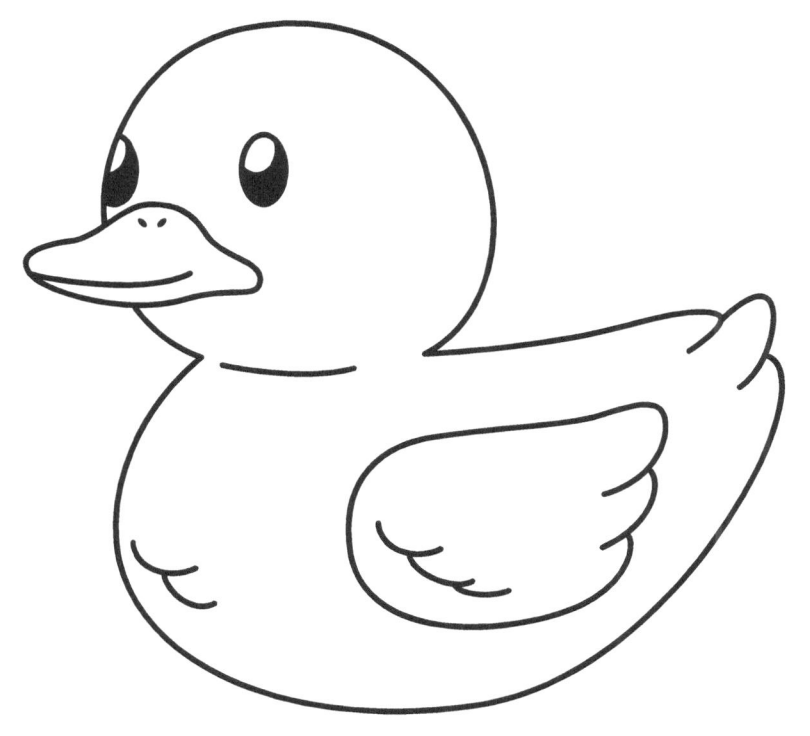

Duck

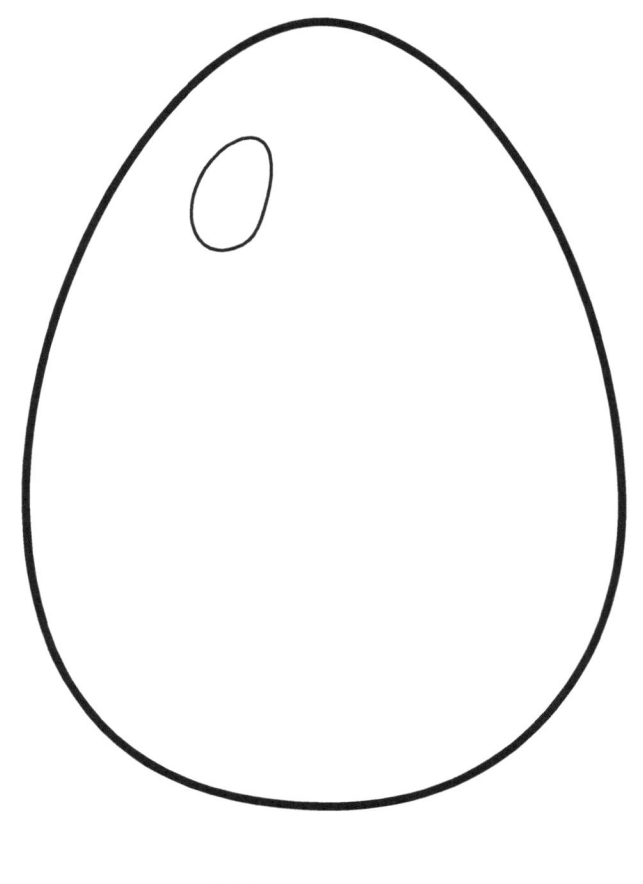

Egg

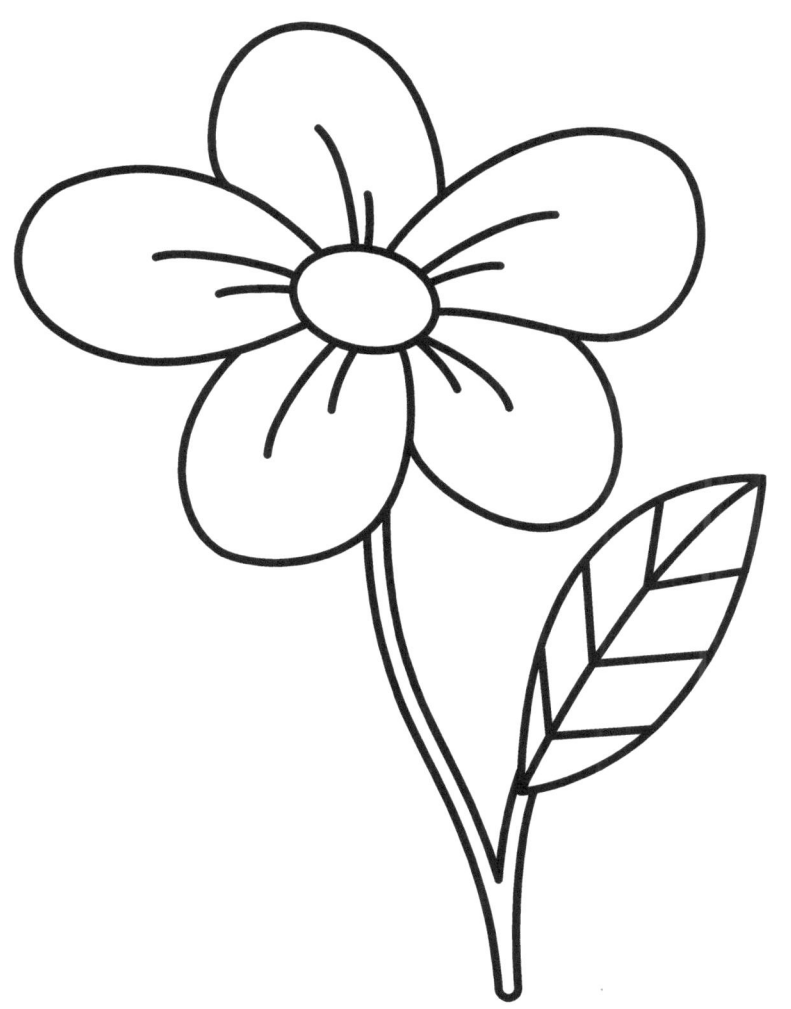

Flower

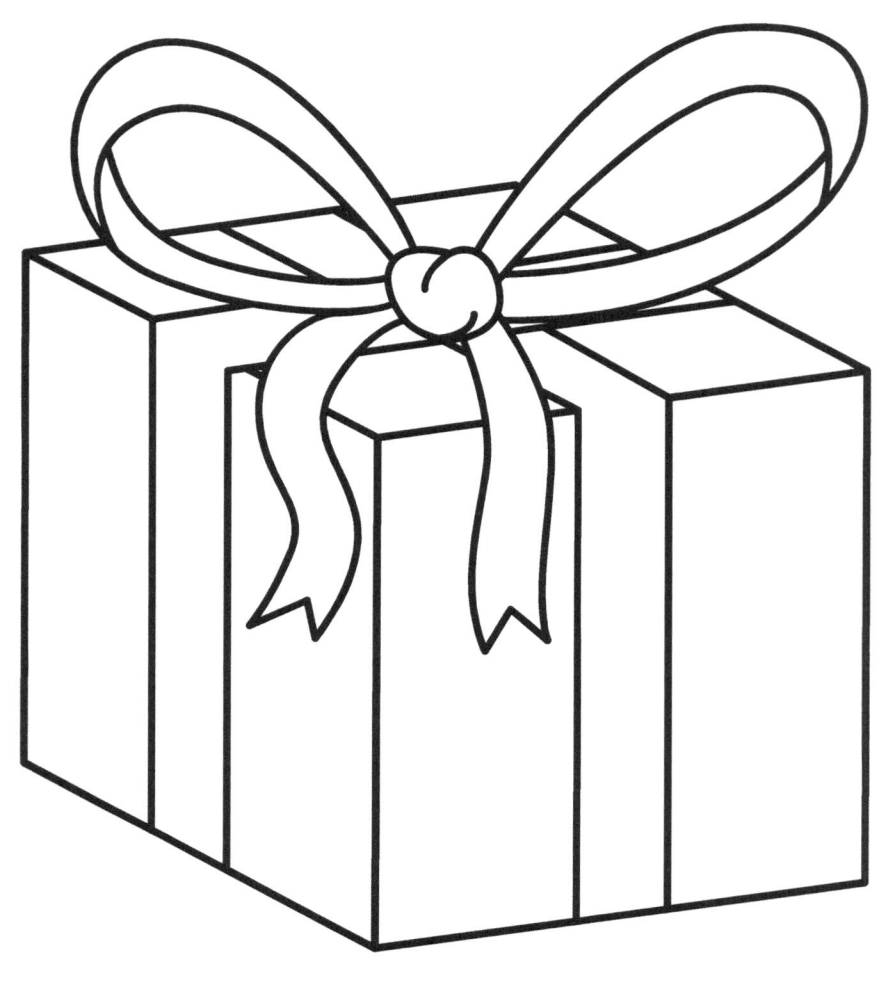

Gift

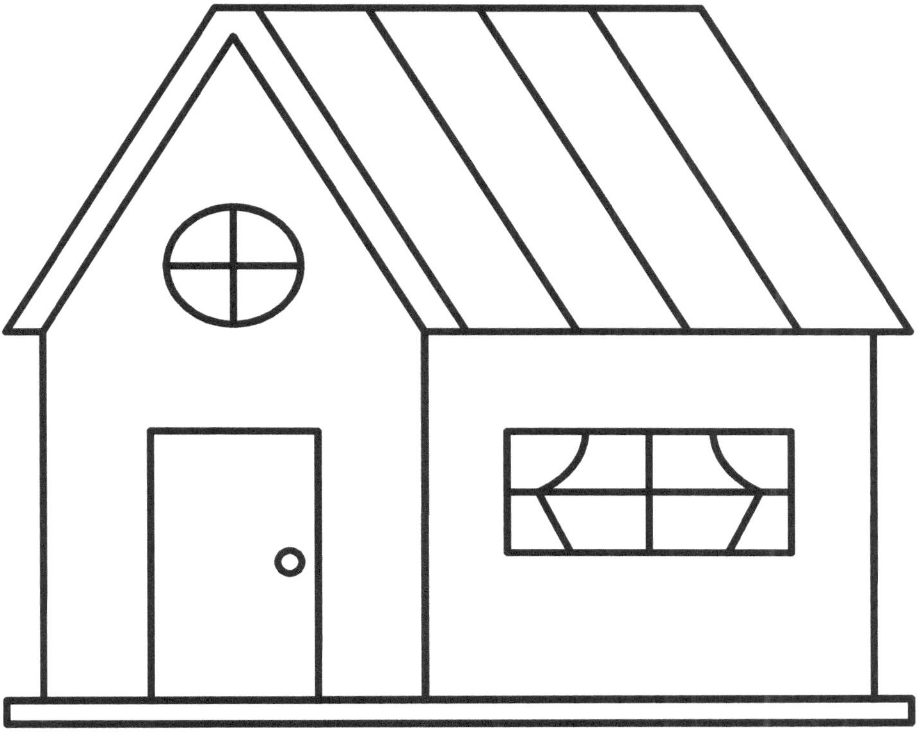

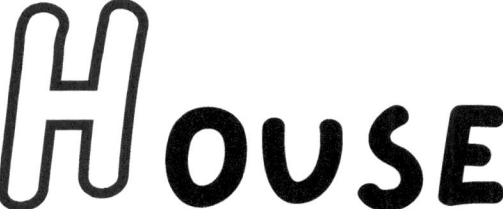

House

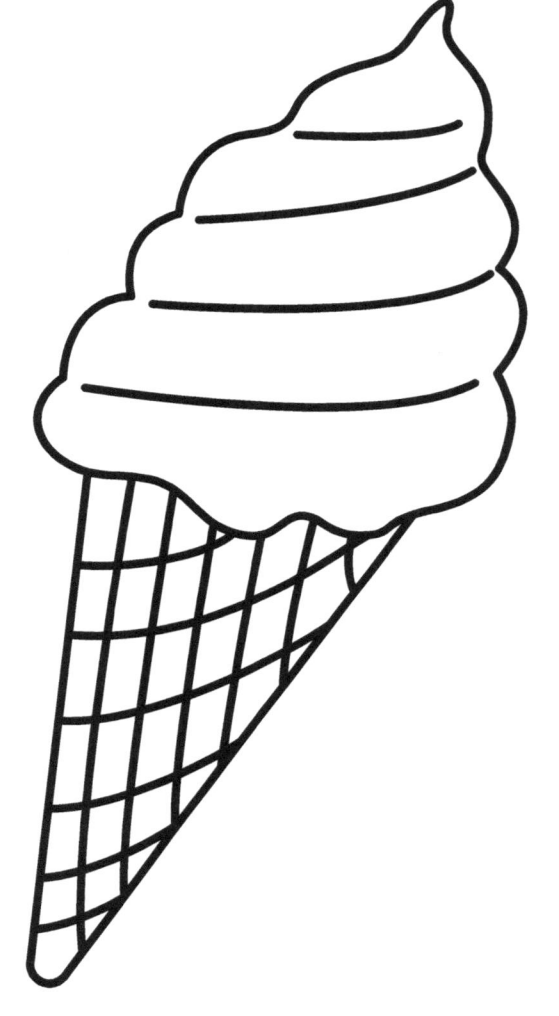

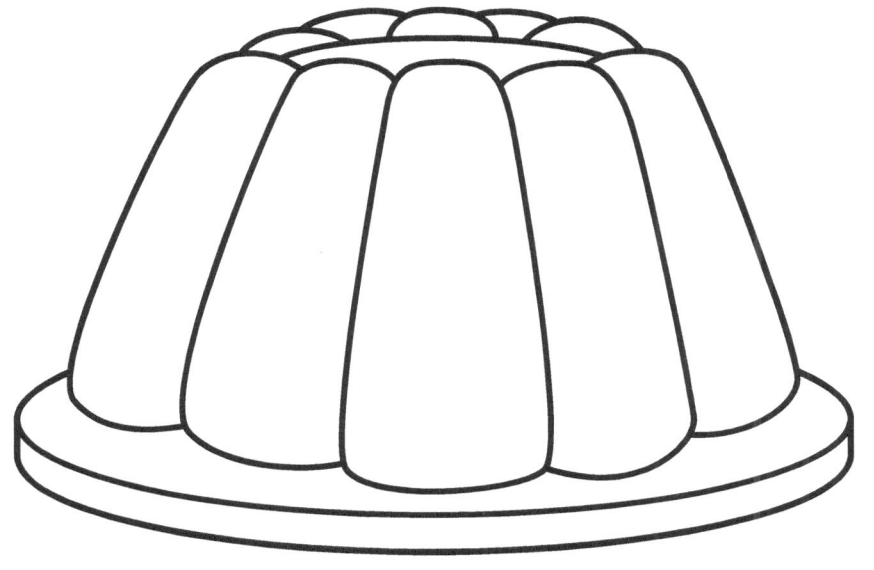

Jelly

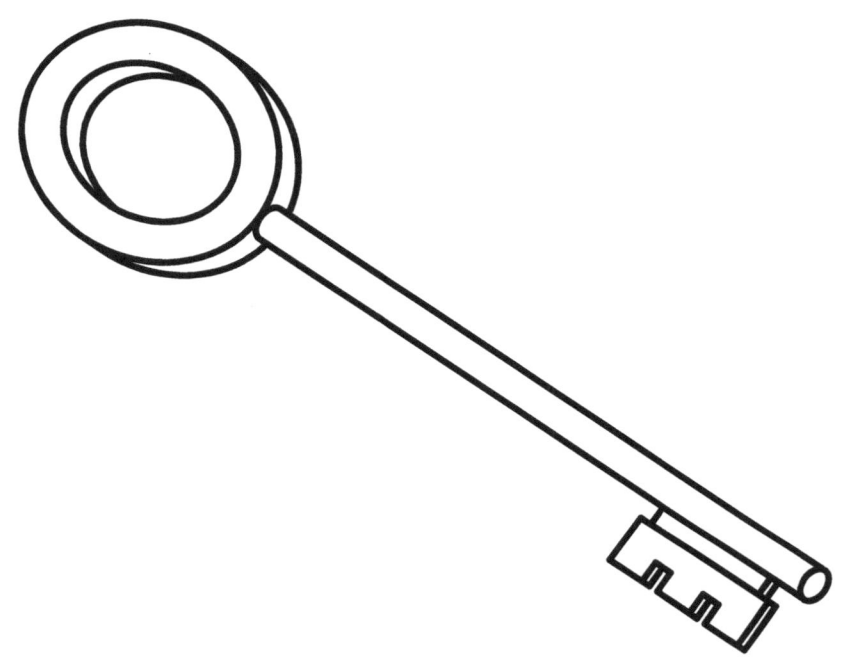

Key

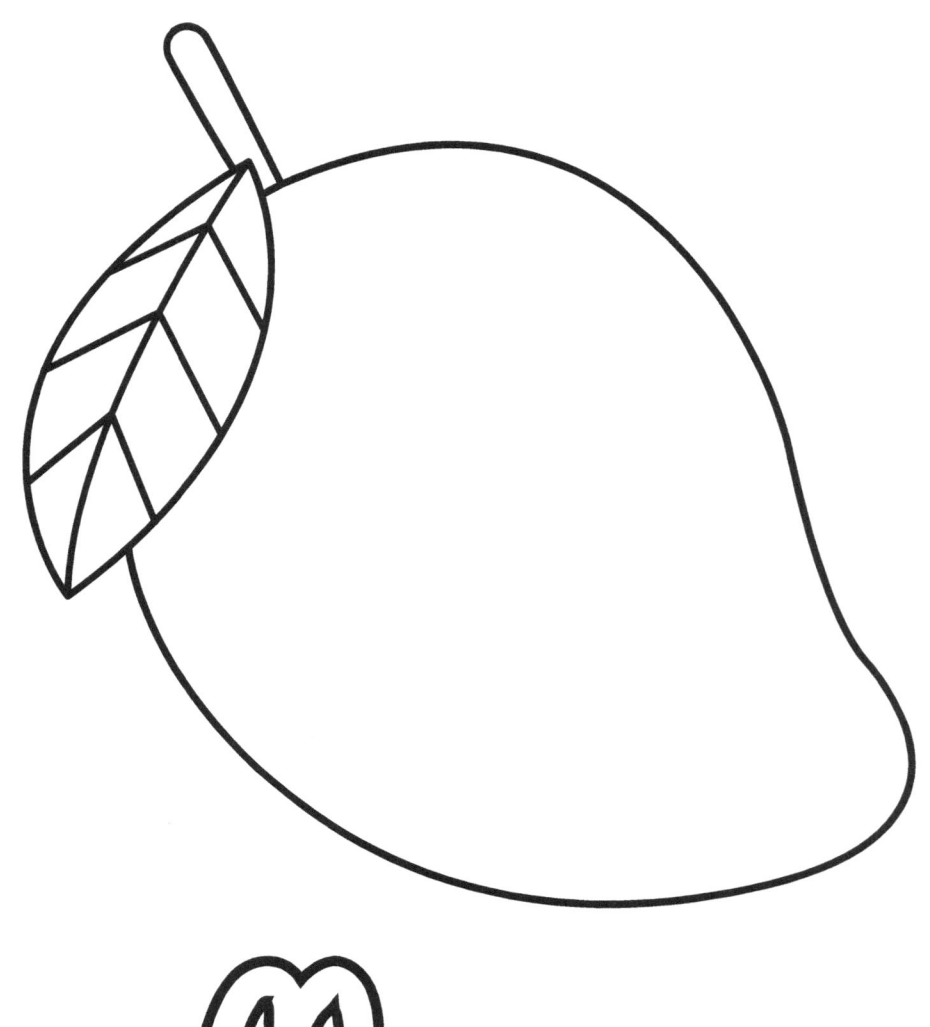

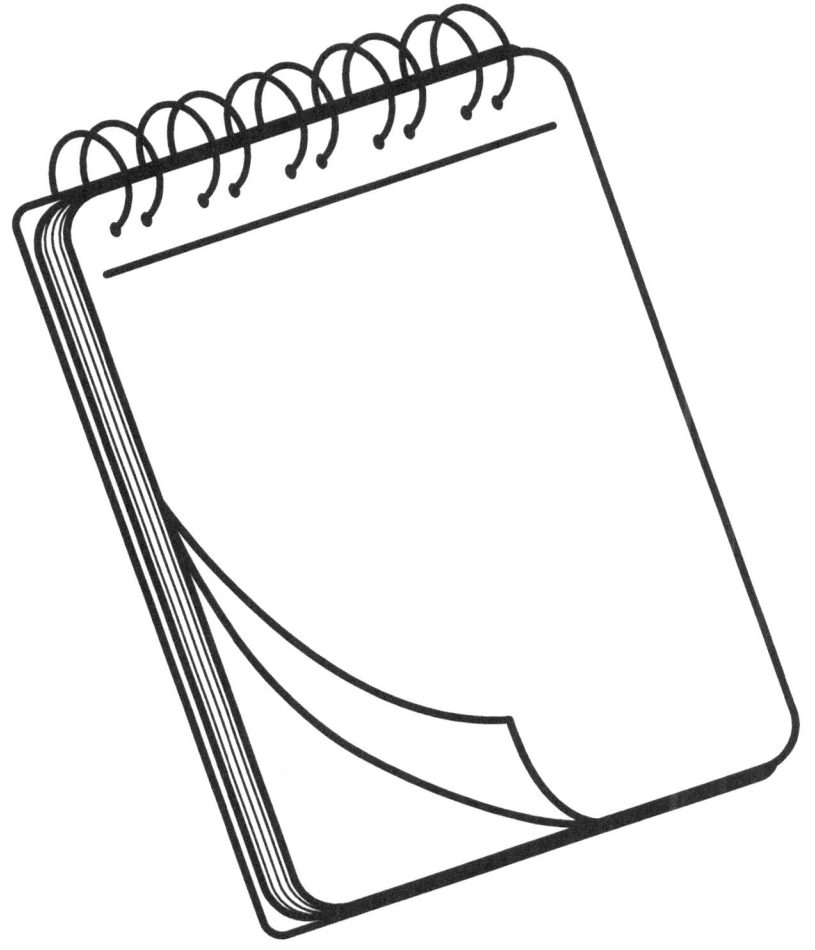

Notepad

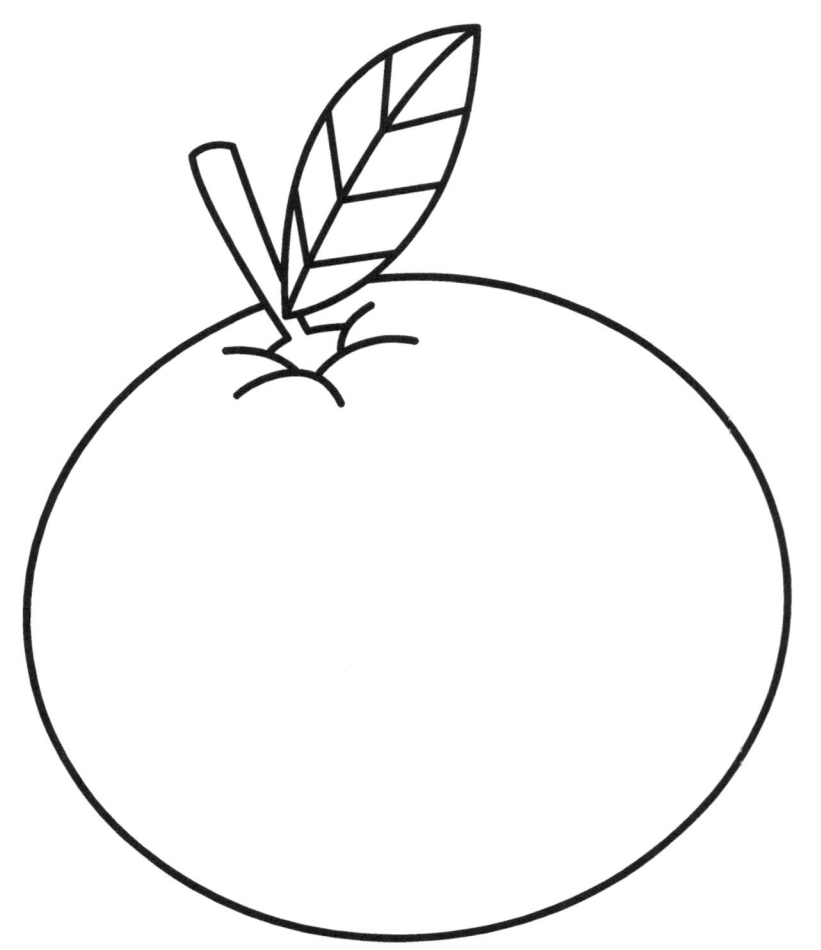

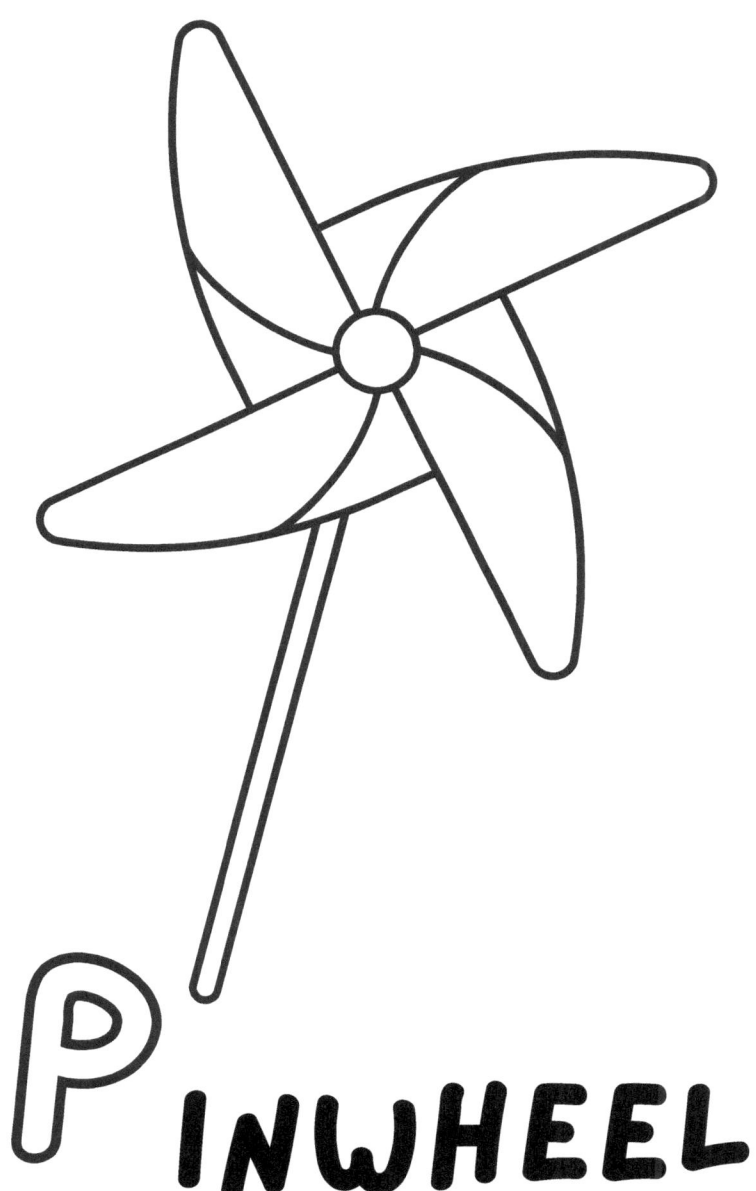

Pinwheel

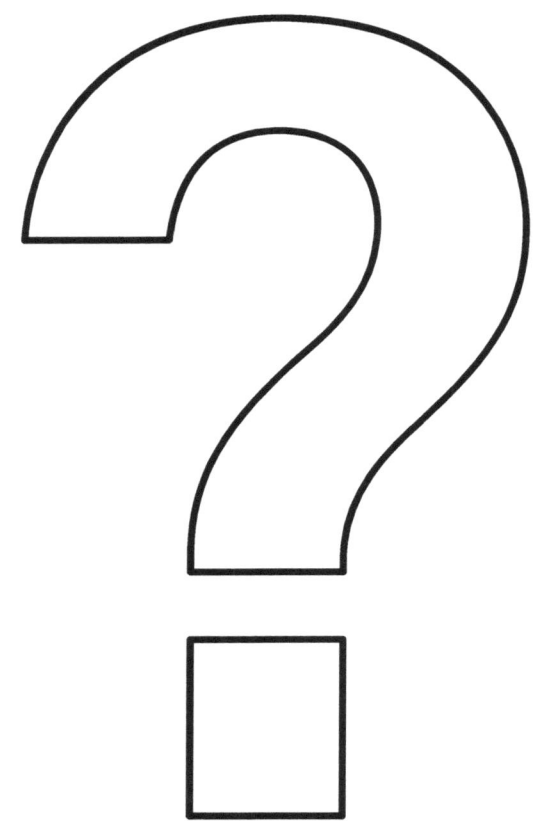

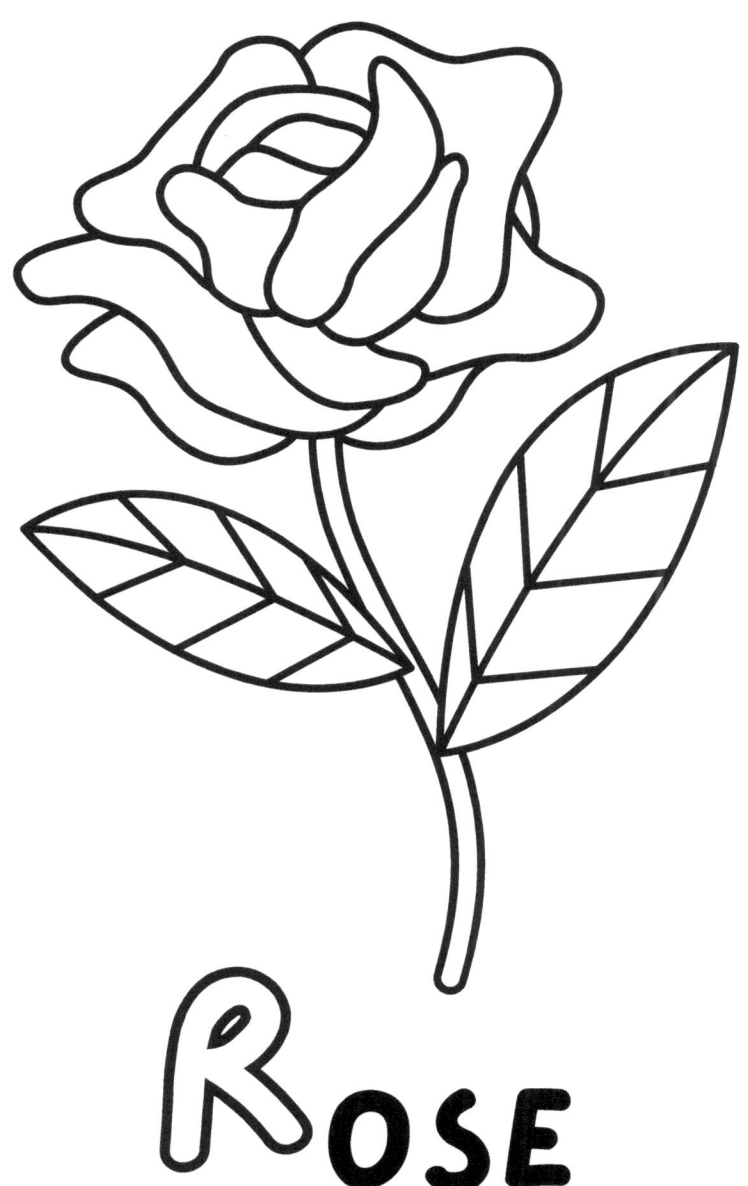

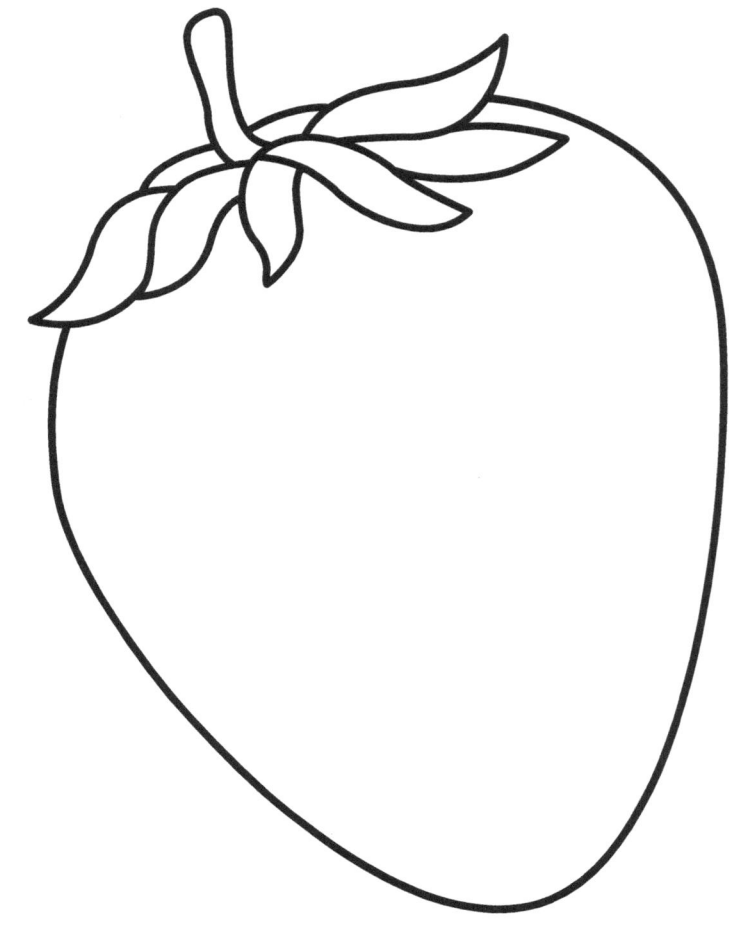

Strawberry

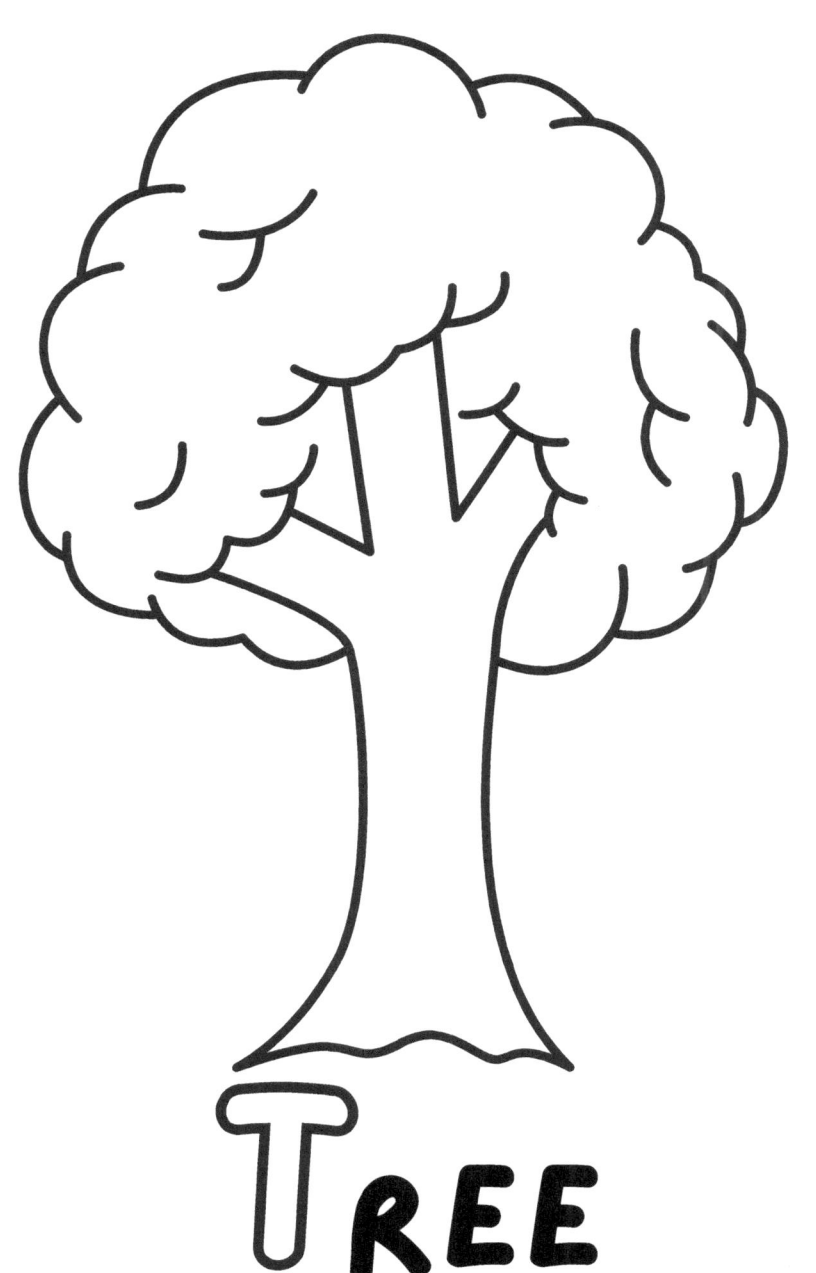

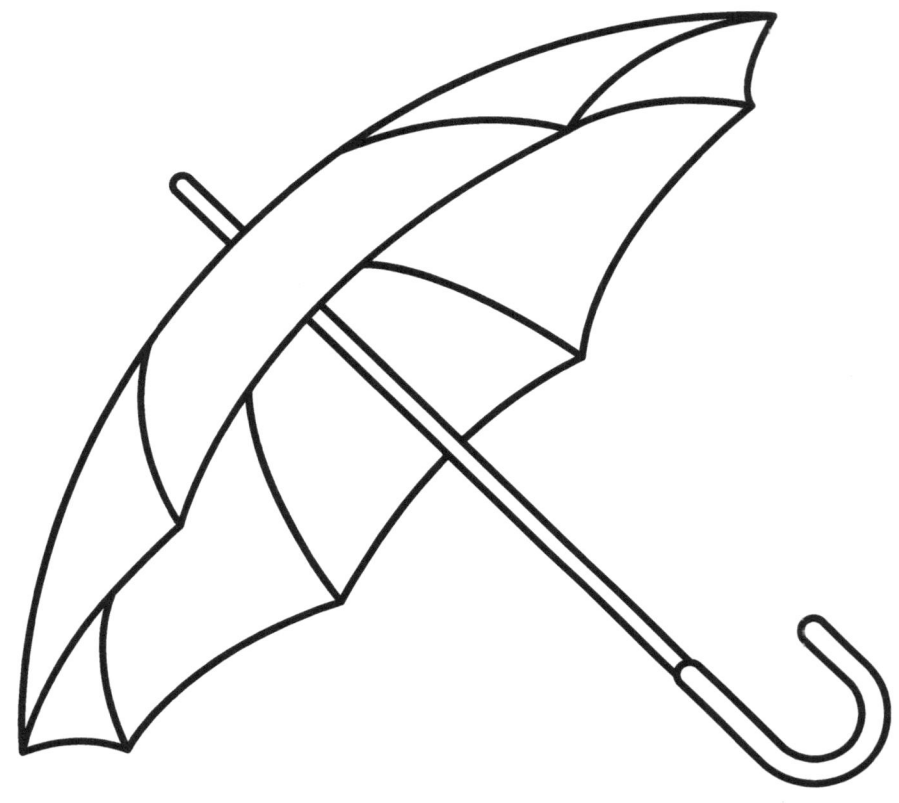

Umbrella

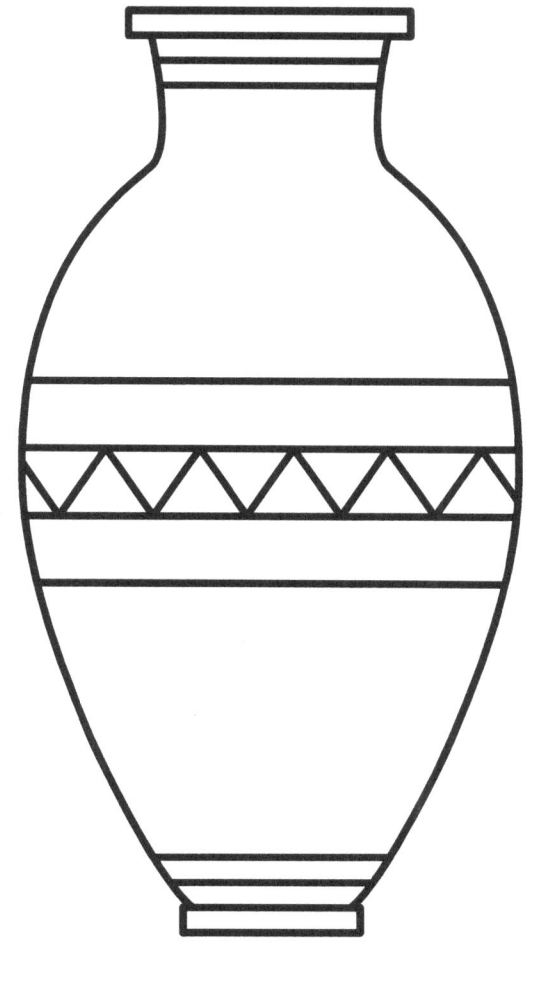

Vase

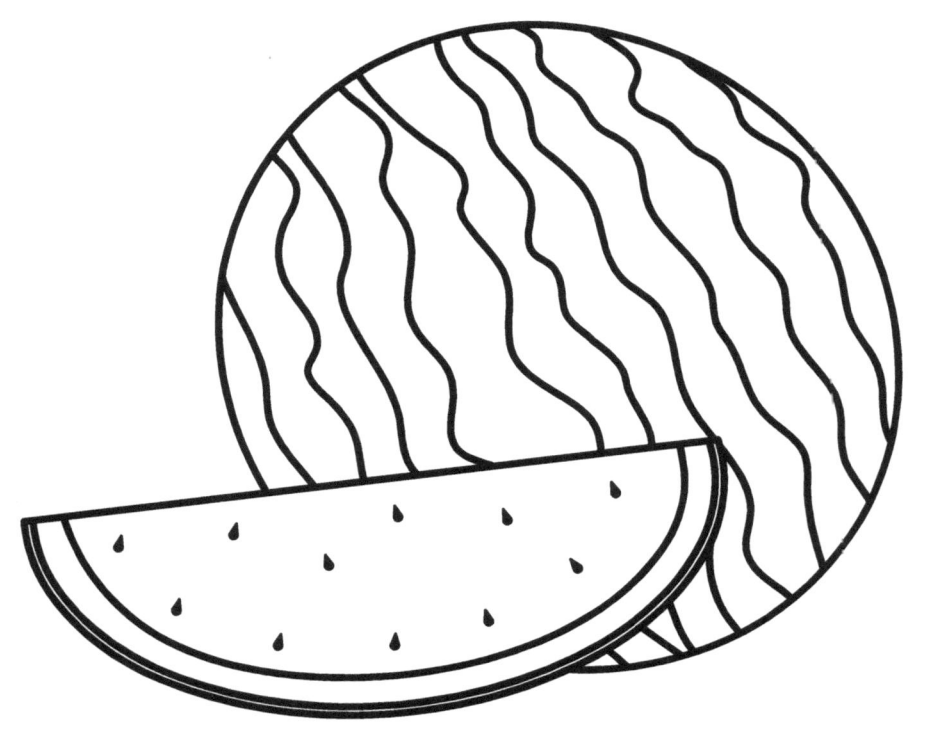

Watermelon

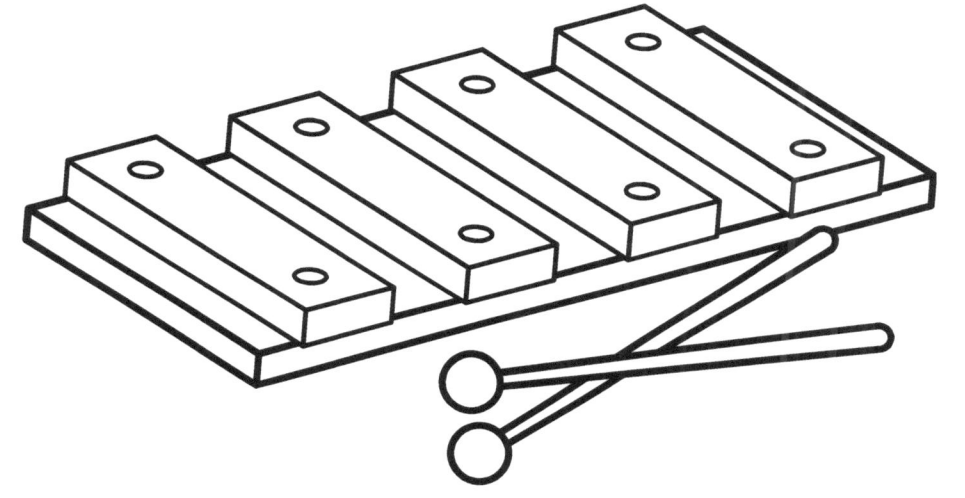

Xylophone

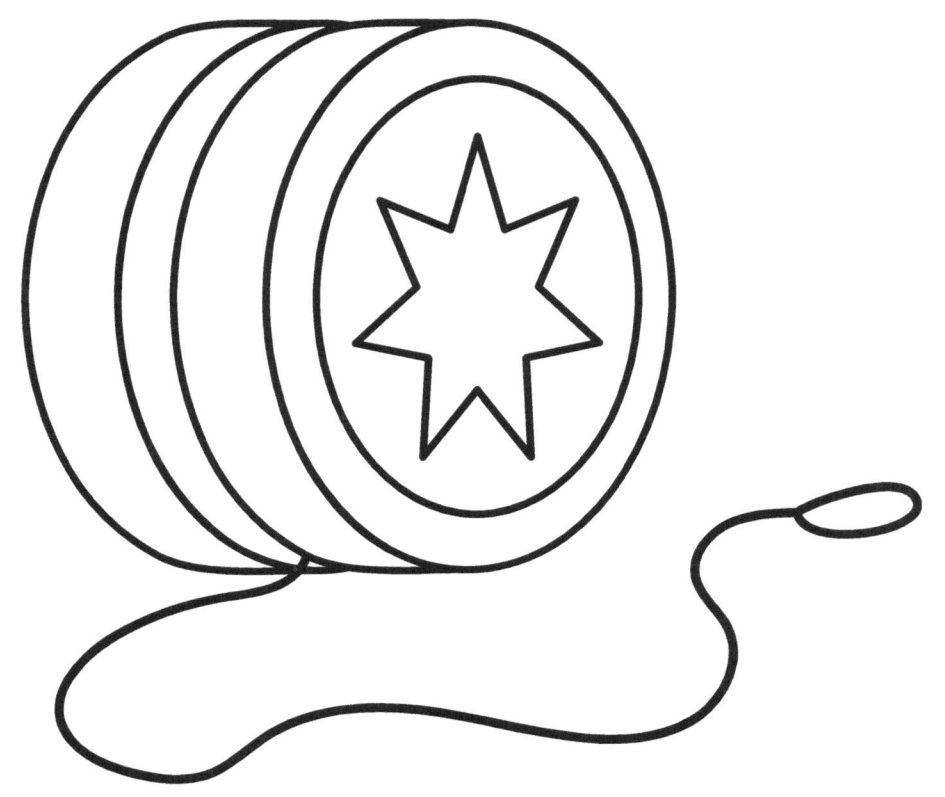

Yoyo

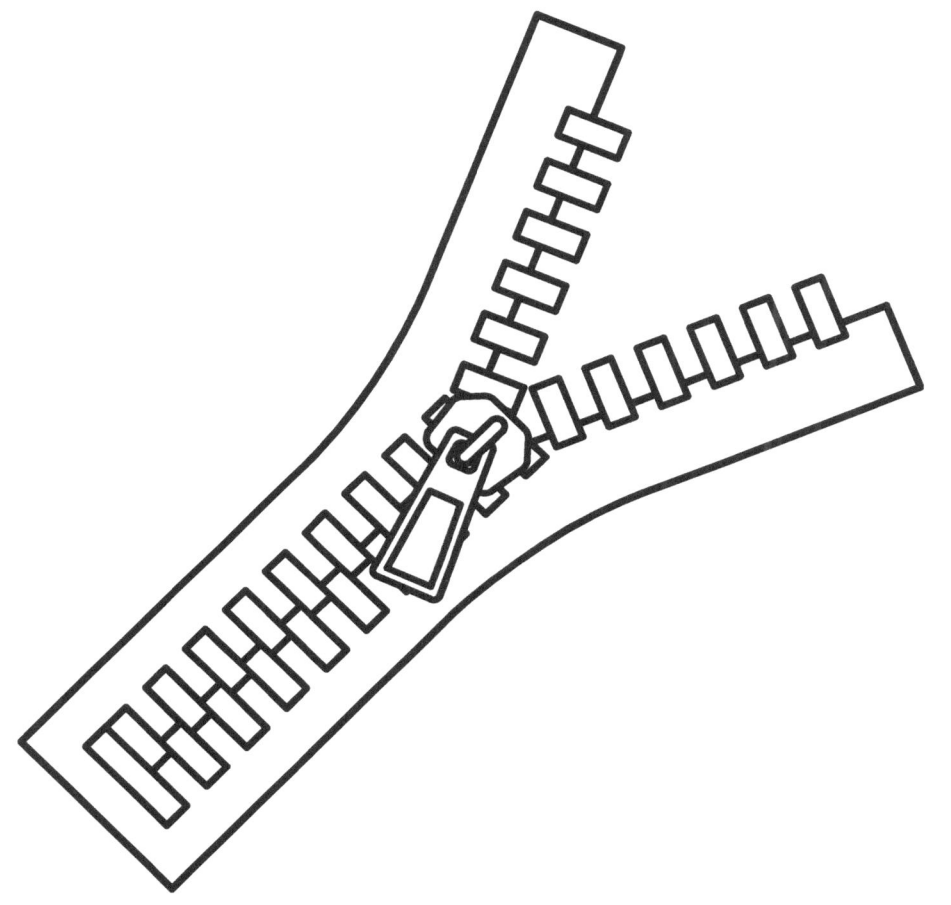

Zipper

www.ingramcontent.com/pod-product-compliance
Lightning Source LLC
Chambersburg PA
CBHW040304220526
45473CB00002B/582